ANIMALS
Who Have Won Our Hearts

ANIMALS
Who Have Won Our Hearts

BY JEAN CRAIGHEAD GEORGE

illustrated by Christine Herman Merrill

A TRUMPET CLUB SPECIAL EDITION

To Carol Ann

—J.C.G.

To my mom, Louise S. Donahue

—C.H.M

The illustrator wishes to thank the following for providing reference material for the drawings and paintings in this book: "The Three Gray Whales": Bill Hess, Editor, *The Open Lead Magazine* ❋ "Koko": Francine Patterson, The Gorilla Foundation ❋ "Smokey Bear": Forest Service, U. S. Department of Agriculture ❋ "The Hemlock Pair": Peter Nye and Michael Allen

Published by The Trumpet Club, Inc.,
a subsidiary of Bantam Doubleday Dell Publishing Group, Inc.,
1540 Broadway, New York, New York 10036.
"A Trumpet Club Special Edition" with the portrayal of a trumpet
and two circles is a registered trademark of
Bantam Doubleday Dell Publishing Group, Inc.

ISBN 0-440-83783-9

This edition published by arrangement with HarperCollins Publishers.

Printed in the United States of America
February 1996
1   3   5   7   9   10   8   6   4   2
UPR

Typography by Christine Hoffman.
The full-color illustrations in this book were painted with oil on canvas.
The black-and-white illustrations were drawn with charcoal pencil on Canson drawing paper.

Contents

Preface vi

BALTO—*Indomitable Sled Dog* 1

PUNXSUTAWNEY PHIL—*The King of Groundhog Day* 7

THE PACING WHITE MUSTANG—*Fastest Horse in the West* 11

SMOKEY BEAR—*A National Symbol* 15

SCANNON—*Lewis and Clark's Resourceful Mascot* 19

THE THREE GRAY WHALES—*Persevering Captives of the Ice* 23

SUGAR—*Cross-Country Traveler* 31

BLIND TOM—*Working Hero of the Railroad* 37

KOKO—*Smart Signing Gorilla* 41

THE HEMLOCK PAIR—*A Living National Emblem* 49

Bibliography 54

Preface

Long ago a slave named Aesop saw human qualities in animals and captured these traits in his fables of morals for people. So famous are "The Tortoise and the Hare" and "The Fox and the Grapes" that they have survived more than two thousand years of telling and retelling. Aesop's animals are lovable and amusing. They are also selfish, greedy and evil, but they tell us more about ourselves than about the animals.

Today we see animals differently. Studies of their behavior enable us to appreciate their innate qualities and to understand where these qualities fit in the scheme of things. And so we have learned that each bird and beast is perfect in its own niche and wonderful to behold.

Like people, some animals are more outstanding than others. Balto, the intelligent sled dog, found his way through a blinding snowstorm using his senses and judgment. We love him for being the best of dogs. The three entrapped whales, air-breathing mammals like us, fought so bravely for breath that our hearts went out to them, and we came to their rescue. Koko learned sign language and showed us just how smart animals really are.

These stories are not fables. They are true stories of individuals who through chance, or the times they lived in—but primarily through their beautiful animalness—became beloved in their own right. —*J.C.G.*

BALTO

Indomitable Sled Dog

Balto, a half-wolf, half-Malamute sled dog, trotted head down in the darkness of a stinging blizzard. Behind him his teammates kept pace as he guided them into Nome, Alaska, and down a deserted street to the hospital.

"Halt!" Musher Gunnar Kasson croaked through ice-burned lips. Balto dropped in the deep snow at the door of the hospital. Kasson sank to his knees beside him. With tears welling from his near-blinded eyes, hands shaking from exhaustion, he pulled sharp chunks of ice from Balto's bleeding paws.

"Balto," Kasson whispered into his neck fur. "Damn fine dog!"

It was 5:30 A.M. on February 2, 1925. Balto had saved lives.

Balto and his ten harness mates were the last in a relay of dog teams that had run the 660-mile trail from Nenana, 350 miles north of Anchorage, to Nome. They carried a consignment of the diphtheria antitoxin that would stop the "black death" that was killing a person a day in the subarctic town. When the railroad train carrying the serum had become snowbound in Nenana, and the planes could not take off, the U.S. Signal Corps sent out a call for dog teams.

Mushers responded. Dangerous as the assignment was, they brought their strongest and most intelligent dogs to the snowbound outposts along the route to Nome. At one post after another, a team would pull in, the serum would be passed on and another team would pull out.

The relay ran day and night for four days. Then Charlie Olson and his team of seven pulled into Bluff, 67½ miles from Nome, in a roaring blizzard. He handed Gunnar Kasson the serum and warned him about the winds and cold.

Kasson decided to wait out the storm; but when, at ten o'clock that night, the blizzard showed no sign of stopping or

even letting up, he took off into the icy tempest.

The next relay point was 34 miles away. As Balto led his team across the Topok River, an 80-mile-an-hour wind struck like a railroad engine and lifted clouds of snow into the air. Neither the dogs nor Kasson could see.

But Balto never hesitated. He trotted on, following his own internal compass that guided him around drifts and out onto an ice-covered lagoon.

Near the shore, Kasson sensed trouble. "Haw," he called. Obeying reluctantly, Balto ran to the left, off the trail, and splashed into an overflow of water. Wet feet meant crippled dogs. In desperation Kasson drove the team into soft snow to dry their paws—and was instantly lost in whiteness.

Not Balto. Picking his way, and making intelligent decisions, he trotted on at a steady pace. Twice the sled dumped and the dogs tangled. Twice Kasson righted the sled, straightened the traces, and let Balto lead the way. Fortunately, as they crossed Norton Sound, the wind got behind them and they covered the next 12½ miles to Port Safety in eighty minutes.

The lights were out at the relay station. Time would be lost arousing the musher and dogs. Twenty-one miles away people were dying. His dogs were running well. "Hup! Hup!" Kasson called, and Balto kept going.

Along the seacoast the snow stopped and Kasson could see again. Two of his dogs were stiffening up. The temperature was thirty-six degrees below zero Fahrenheit. He stopped to make rabbitskin boots for the Malamutes, and went on.

When at last they pulled into Nome, exhausted but undaunted, the dog relay teams had completed in five and a half days a trip that usually took the mail train more than twenty-five days.

The next morning Balto's name appeared on the front page of every major newspaper in the United States. He was praised on the floor of Congress. Invitations for personal appearances poured in. Balto and Kasson toured from California to New York, stopping in big and little towns amid cheers and fanfare.

Balto has not been forgotten. His statue, made by R. G. Roth, stands in New York City's Central Park. Under Balto's name are these words:

Dedicated to the indomitable spirit of the sled dogs that relayed antitoxins 660 miles over rough ice, across treacherous waters, through Arctic blizzards from Nenana to the relief of stricken Nome in the Winter of 1925.

PUNXSUTAWNEY PHIL

—

The King of Groundhog Day

Every year at two in the morning on February 2, fourteen men in tuxedos, black coats and top hats carry a groundhog named Punxsutawney Phil from the cozy zoo near the library to the top of Gobbler's Knob in Punxsutawney, Pennsylvania. He is placed in a hollow stump that is outfitted with a door. Half awake, he curls in a ball and goes back to sleep. The men drink coffee and wait for daybreak.

February 2 is Groundhog Day. If February 2 is bright and clear, there'll be six more weeks of winter; so says the legend the Romans carried to the Teutons, or Germans, and the Germans carried to America. Since the groundhog is a most intelligent and sensible animal, the Pennsylvania Germans reasoned that he, in his wisdom, would see his shadow and go back to sleep for another six weeks of winter. If not, he would stay up, and spring would come early.

In 1871, on February 2, at a dull time of year when the holidays are over and there was little farming to do, a few Punxsutawneyites hied to the woods to test the legend. They found a groundhog and named him Punxsutawney Phil. He answered their question by going back to sleep, and the townspeople feasted and danced. One hundred and twenty-three years later they are still asking Phil about the weather and dancing.

At 7:30 A.M. the president of the Punxsutawney Groundhog Club taps on the stump and awakens Phil. He is irritated. He has been awakened twice this day, and he sees no carrots. He is handed to the president, chittering angrily. The president chitters back. Visitors hold their breath. They are told the man and the groundhog are talking about the weather. Then over the horizon comes the sun, and Phil's shadow falls on the ground.

"Six more weeks of winter," the president carols. The men march down the hill, the band strikes up, and everyone for miles around celebrates Groundhog Day.

Phil is carried home to his zoo. He is not beautiful. He is stout, his tail is short and bushy, his ears are stubby and one is chewed back. He tucks his head into his belly and goes right back to sleep, as he would do in the wild. Groundhogs hibernate in October and awaken in February to locate mates. Ordinarily, they then go back to sleep and get up in March to breed. The young are born in April. Groundhogs devour gardens, crops, flowers and grass. They are easily tamed. These, like Phil, all love to sit on human laps, mow grass all summer and sleep all winter. They are the perfect pet. But no one is really sure how accurate the weather forecasting is, except for Punxsutawneyites. They say their King of the Weather Prophets has never been wrong.

THE PACING WHITE MUSTANG

Fastest Horse in the West

In the days when there were still buffalos, Native Americans, and U.S. Cavalry on the Great Plains, the Pacing White Mustang lived in wild splendor somewhere "out west." He sped like a tornado across the prairie and commanded his herd like a general. Stories were written about his strength and beauty, and prizes were offered for his capture. But no one could rope him.

His speed was legendary. He moved his front and back legs simultaneously, first on one side and then on the other, in a dynamic gait called "pacing." Other horses alternately put forward the front right with back left legs, then the front left with the back right. The pacer fairly flew.

He was as wild as the cornflower and as beautiful as

snow on the mountains. The Osage Indians said he was a ghost. Cowboys said he was a mirage.

But he was out there and he was real. Washington Irving removed all doubt. In 1832 he sighted the magnificent white stallion while on a tour of the prairies with the Commissioner of Indian Affairs. A few years later an army gen-

eral and one of his captains were awakened by a night battle between wild horses and wolves. At daylight they rode out to catch the horses for the army.

About a mile downstream they came upon the howling wolves and a herd of about 150 horses. Rising above them all, flailing his feet as he commanded, was the Pacing White Mustang. He had formed the mares in a circle facing inward so they could kick the enemy with their hoofs. Protected in-side the circle were the foals and yearlings. What was most extraordinary was that the white mustang ruled the other stallions. At his command they charged the wolves who were attacking the herd.

Upon scenting the men, the wolves ran off, and the men went after the horses. The Pacing White Mustang instantly signaled his stallions. They turned, pawed the ground in front of the mares and neighed. The mares opened their circle. The colts and yearlings ran out and the stallions led them off. The mares followed the colts.

The white stallion brought up the rear and took on the men. He would let a rider come to within twenty yards of him, then pull swiftly away, fall back, and let another horseman approach. In this manner he held off the horse raiders until his herd was out of sight. Then he vanished. Even the disappointed general had to admit that he and all the others who had tried, but had failed, to capture the white stallion had been outsoldiered by the Pacing White Mustang.

SMOKEY BEAR

—

A National Symbol

When the flames were out, when the thunder and crackle of blazing trees had died down, when the worst forest fire in the history of Lincoln National Forest, New Mexico, was over, a badly burned bear cub was clinging to a tree. A weary firefighter snapped his picture, then rescued the hurting and bewildered cub. That was in 1950.

The rangers named him Smokey after the familiar poster character Smokey Bear, a cartoon bear in a ranger's hat and blue jeans holding a shovel. He had been created in 1944 by the U.S. Forest Service with the help of the Advertising Council to publicize a campaign to prevent forest fires. Posters of the cartoon bear read "Only You Can Prevent Forest Fires!" and were tacked up in every national forest

and park as well as in public build-
ings.

Then the real Smokey came along.
The rangers nursed him back to health
and sent him to the National Zoo in
Washington, D.C. Photographs of the
badly burned cub, his frolicsome recovery and his life in Washington sent the popularity of the
cartoon Smokey Bear skyrock-
eting. Congress copyrighted
Smokey's name and image in 1952, and
by 1976 Smokey Bear products had earned the Forest Service
more than $1.5 million in royalties.

With this publicity, the living Smokey Bear became one
of the most popular animals at the National Zoo. Thousands
of visitors dropped by to see the black bear who limped on
his stiff leg and still bore scars from the fire that some care-
less camper or smoker had started. Smokey's misfortune be-

came the best reason for preventing forest fires. He even made public appearances. Eventually he had his own Smokey Bear fan club. Membership was in the many thousands. Children who signed up to be Junior Forest Rangers received not only a Ranger kit but an official-looking badge and pictures of the real and the cartoon Smokeys.

In May 1975, when he was twenty-five years old (which is equal to seventy in human years), the National Zoo and the Forest Service retired Smokey in an impressive ceremony in which they introduced Smokey Junior, another orphan of a fire in Lincoln National Forest. Smokey Senior died a year later. His remains were buried at the Smokey Bear Historical Park in Lincoln National Forest, but his message lives on: "Only You Can Prevent Forest Fires."

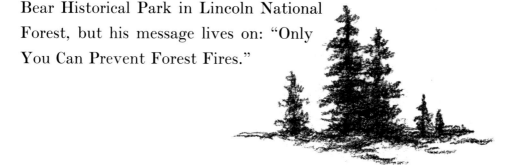

SCANNON

—

Lewis and Clark's Resourceful Mascot

Bred for the noble purpose of rescuing people at sea, Scannon, a large, lovable Newfoundland dog, defied his heredity to become a food gatherer, a retriever, a bear dog and a collector of biological specimens.

He belonged to Meriwether Lewis, captain of the Lewis and Clark Expedition sent out by President Thomas Jefferson in May 1804. The expedition would determine if the Missouri and Columbia rivers could provide a water route across North America to the rich Northwest. Scannon, mascot of the expedition, sensed his job was more than looking handsome. He caught squirrels for food, drowned a wolf and was seriously wounded by the beaver he caught for Lewis's collection of wildlife. The collection

had been requested by President Jefferson.

The expedition was far up the Missouri River when Scannon's wounds were healed. Migrating geese settled down on the river by the thousands. Scannon jumped into the water and caught one after another for the table. Game was not always easy to come by, and the crew rewarded Scannon's spectacular efforts with high praise. The attention was so heady that the big dog was inspired to greater feats. He drove human-killing grizzly bears out of camp in the Yellowstone River region and took on a bull buffalo that thundered across the Missouri and into the midst of the sleeping crew on the ground. Barking and herding like a sheepdog, he maneuvered the bull around men in sleeping bags and back across the Missouri River.

Calling on the talents of all breeds of dogs, Scannon rode in boats, tracked, retrieved, killed snakes, dug into holes to collect what lived there, and arrived with his master in good health at the Pacific Coast on January 6, 1806. There Scannon hunted elk and collected wildlife until it was time to start back to St. Louis in March.

Still performing his self-imposed duties, Scannon arrived in St. Louis on September 23, 1806, together with all the men but one, who had died of appendicitis. As Scannon jumped ashore, he completed a journey that some historians consider the most successful and intelligent expedition in history. Eventually the route would bind the east and the west together as the United States of America.

Scannon knew nothing of this. He and his master were home.

THE THREE GRAY WHALES

—

Persevering Captives of the Ice

For twenty-one days three gray whales fought for life and breath in the frozen Beaufort Sea, while television viewers around the world watched them in pain and hope.

Bone, Bonnet and Crossbeak, three endangered California gray whales, had left the Arctic Ocean at the end of summer and were on their way to Baja California, Mexico, to breed and winter. Feeding close to shore at Point Barrow, Alaska, they lingered too long and were surrounded by ice on October 7, 1988. That evening an Eskimo hunter found the air-breathing sea mammals about two hundred yards from shore, struggling for breath in an opening in the ice.

He reported the plight of the whales to the biologists at the North Slope Borough Wildlife Management Department in Barrow. Both Eskimo and white scientists thought perhaps the whales should be put out of their misery. Then television got hold of the story and they wondered no more. Letters and phone calls poured in. The world wanted the three gray whales rescued.

Eskimo hunters together with the scientists set out to do so. Using chain saws, they cut a series of breathing holes leading toward open water three miles away. When this effort was shown on television, six-foot chain saws were sent to the rescuers by concerned businesspeople. A National Guard helicopter arrived with a five-ton chunk of concrete to drop on the ice to make more holes with less human effort. It didn't work. The rescuers went on sawing. As the days grew colder, the holes refroze. At their own expense, several people hopped a plane and arrived in Barrow with costly de-icing equipment.

The de-icers kept the water open for the whales, and the rescuers sawed on. Then something went wrong. The whales stopped using the holes.

The Eskimos got down on their bellies and talked to the whales as their ancestors had done for centuries. They urged them to use the holes. The whales seemed to understand that the men were helping them and swam to a hole, only to turn around and go back.

Then Malek, an elderly Eskimo hunter, spoke to the whales. After a while he reported to the rescuers: "The water is too shallow, the whales are saying." The scientists took a sounding of the lagoon bottom and found that the whales were right. A shoal was blocking the escape route. The water was too shallow under the breathing holes.

Urgently the men cut holes leading around the shoal, and urgently the whales responded. They swam from one hole to the next in great excitement as they moved toward the open sea.

On the eighteenth day of the rescue attempt, the holes stretched one and a half miles toward freedom, but the whales were growing weary. Bone, the smallest, disappeared and was never seen again.

That night a wind moved great floes of ice toward Point Barrow and piled them in a ridge twenty feet high. It grounded the ridge on the bottom of the lagoon and cut off all escape. The next morning, when Bonnet and Crossbeak were surfacing to breathe, Malek again went to the whales. He knew they did not need to eat, for they had been feeding in the Beaufort Sea all summer, storing fat for their long migration. But they were under stress and losing weight. They needed a friend. Day and night he remained with the gray whales, soothing them with his voice and stroking their ice-torn noses with his hands.

The rescuers sawed on toward the ridge while National

Guard helicopters brought supplies and camera operators. Meanwhile around the world, television watchers turned on their sets each morning to see if the whales were still alive. At the White House's direction, the Air Force assigned a C-5A Galaxy to ferry more equipment to Barrow. The President of the United States wished the whales well.

Then the Soviet Union responded. The cold-war enemy of the United States announced that two Soviet icebreakers three hundred miles from Barrow were on their way to help the whales.

Encouraged, the American rescuers sawed furiously forward, trying to reach the ridge in time to meet the Soviet icebreakers. Again the whales stopped swimming. This time the men knew why—shallow water. Since they were about five hundred feet from the ridge, they cut a big pool for the whales and went back to town to sleep and to wait for the Soviets—all but Malek. He stayed with the whales all night, stroking and calming them.

In the darkness of the morning of October 26, the rescue crew returned to watch the Soviet icebreakers cut a path through the ridge as if it were butter. The whales bolted for open water. Cheers went up, and it was reported that the whales were free.

They were not. They could not surface to breathe in the ice-jammed track. They came back to the last hole. Once more the Soviets cut through the ice. The whales moved but went the wrong way. They returned to the hole and thrust their heads above water. Malek talked to them, pointed them in the right direction and gave them a shove. With that, Bonnet and Crossbeak rose halfway out of the water in a breach, dove and disappeared.

The Soviet captain saw one pass his ship. At last the whales were free.

SUGAR

—

Cross-Country Traveler

Like any cat, Sugar, a part-Persian house pet, lived in her own secret world. She followed her night trails into the countryside, she met up with friends and enemies unknown to her owners and she withdrew to sunning spots to purr or not to purr, depending on her whim.

But unlike any other cat, Sugar was endowed with an uncanny sense of geography, and she would go down in the annals of science as the cat who was "guided by a still unrecognized means of knowing."*

When she was several years old, Sugar walked into the Woodses' farmhouse in California. Her long, creamy hair and copper eyes provoked admiration, and she soon had bowls of

*J. B. Rhine & S. R. Feather, *Journal of Parapsychology*, 1962.

cream and bits of fish set before her. She also demanded affection, and when Mrs. Woods picked her up to stroke her beautiful fur and say nice things to her, her fingers found a deformity in Sugar's left hip. It did not seem to interfere with the cat's stride or agility, but it was there.

Sugar did not leave. She took up the cat role of mouser and patrolled the Woodses' property. Gradually she bonded not with the house, as do most cats, but with Mr. and Mrs. Woods. The relationship between them deepened over the years. The only problem Sugar presented her owners was that she would not ride in cars. They could not take her on vacations; they could not take her on visits to family and friends. Sugar seemed to be saying to them that her deformed hip was due to an automobile accident. But they could not know. Sugar brought them mice and crickets, told them with a "meow" that she was hungry, or with a "merow" that she wanted the door opened, but where she came from and what had happened to her remained her secret.

Then came the crisis. The Woodses had the opportunity

to move to a farm in Oklahoma, and they did not turn it down. Feeling that it would be cruel to force Sugar to ride fifteen hundred miles in a car, they did what they thought best. They gave Sugar to a neighbor who was eager to have her. Although they would miss her, they knew she had a good home, and they drove away satisfied that Sugar would be happy.

Two weeks after the Woodses left California, Sugar disappeared.

Fourteen months later, Mrs. Woods was in her barn working when a part-Persian cat leaped through the window and landed softly on her shoulder.

Mrs. Woods took her in her arms. She saw the cream-colored fur and the copper eyes. Then she ran her fingers over the hip.

"Sugar," she said. "It's you!"

Mrs. Woods called her friend in California. "Yes," she said, "Sugar did run away."

No one had given her a ride; no one had reported seeing her. Sugar had crossed fifteen hundred miles of deserts and mountains. She had passed through or around towns. She had eaten well, avoided cars, and had somehow found the Woodses on their new farm in Oklahoma. Sugar's story would be hard to believe if Mr. and Mrs. Woods hadn't

known that they had left Sugar in California and that she had arrived a year and two months later on their Oklahoma farm.

Even now, scientists and parapsychologists at Duke University wonder what signals from the earth Sugar listened to in her long journey across the southwestern United States.

Sugar kept these secrets to herself, too.

BLIND TOM

—

Working Hero of the Railroad

Blind Tom, a strong, dignified gelding, stood in the midst of the well-dressed dignitaries who were celebrating the completion of the first transcontinental railroad on May 10, 1869. He had been invited to the party not by the governors and railroad company presidents, but by the men who had worked with him. Rugged ironmen, spikers and gandy dancers had escorted their friend and companion in labor to the top of Promontory Point, Utah, to take his rightful place in history.

He was one of more than twenty-five thousand horses and mules that had powered supply wagons and hauled railroad ties, dirt, rocks and food to build the great iron road. On this day of glory he was there to represent them.

The construction of the railroad was one of the most ferocious races in American history. The Central Pacific was building eastward from the border of California, the Union Pacific westward from Omaha, Nebraska. The rail company that covered the most territory would win the most land and business. Men and horses were pressed to their limits.

Blind Tom went to work on the first day of construction when "Hell on Wheels," a massive city of work cars, pulled out from Omaha. He was still working at the same job twenty-seven months later when the two railroad companies met on May 10.

He worked in darkness. Some say the snow had blinded him; others say it was the prairie dust. Whatever the

tragedy that had befallen him, he did not let it interfere with his work. His job was to haul the heavy flatcar of iron rails and spikes from "Hell on Wheels" to the ironmen, spikers and gandy dancers waiting at the end of the track. It was a strenuous job, and he never once balked. He hauled every rail in the eleven hundred miles of Union Pacific road bed. No other horse helped him.

He was obedient to the job even when bands of Cheyenne, Sioux and Crow Indians swept around him, stealing horses and derailing trains. Ears forward, head down, he would plod on toward the men who were waiting for him in the hot, dry land of Nebraska and Wyoming.

"Where is Blind Tom today?" the railroad workers would ask, to find out how much trail they had laid.

On that day in May 1869, Blind Tom listened to the famous gold spike being hammered into the last clamp to end the Herculean endeavor of building a transcontinental railroad. Then he leaned down and cropped the Utah grasses. Horse power in America had come to an end.

KOKO

Smart Signing Gorilla

"Fine animal gorilla," said a young gorilla, Koko, in American Sign Language. A door to the silent world of the animals had been opened.

Using sign language and eventually a talking computer, Koko—under the devoted tutelage of her "mother," Francine (Penny) Patterson—has told us what it is like to be a gorilla. It is just as frustrating and pleasant as being a human being.

Koko was born July 4, 1971, in the San Francisco Zoo. Penny saw the infant three months later and knew what she wanted to do for a graduate study: She would teach Koko to speak in sign language. After another month the zoo and Stanford University agreed to let her try, and a most remarkable experiment began. It demonstrated that gorillas, which have no vocal cords, can nevertheless use language. With sign language Koko expressed her inner emotions. "This gentle animal," Penny wrote, "feels all the emotions you and I experience; grief, hope, greed, generosity, shame, love and hate."

Koko's first word was "drink," the hand made into a fist with the thumb up, then put to the mouth. When that got her a bottle of milk, she quickly learned more signs. One lesson later, she signed "food" and Penny fed her. Koko was so pleased that she put a bucket over her head and ran around wildly. Two months later, when her vocabulary had expanded to eight words and combinations of those

words, Penny wrote that Koko did "something simple but
somehow very touching." She took Penny gently by the
hand and led her around her room, pausing frequently to ad-
just the position of their hands.

Gorillas have long been known to be moody and Koko
was no exception. She was a very stubborn youngster. It
took her two long months to learn the word for "egg," which
she disliked, and one minute to learn "berry." She loved to
eat berries.

A sense of humor often rose out of her stubbornness.
When asked the color of her white towel for a boring
umpteenth time, she signed "red." When asked twice again,

she replied "red," then carefully picked a tiny speck of red lint off her towel. She chuckled, and again said "red."

Koko turned the pages of picture books and named the animals, recognized herself in photographs and in the mirror, carefully cleaned her room, and played with her pets. So deeply did she grieve when her cat died that she was allowed to choose a new kitten from a litter. She took care of it with gentleness and love.

Eventually Penny purchased Koko from the zoo and moved her and her trailer to the Stanford campus. At the end of moving day, Koko signed, "Go home." When this request was not fulfilled, she sobbed the tearless cry of the gorilla.

As Koko learned more words, she was able to express

not only her likes, but her dislikes. She hated the noisy blue jays at the zoo, so she called people who annoyed her "bird." One day when Kate, an assistant, would not open the refrigerator, Koko signed, "Kate bird rotten." When truly angry she had a humdinger of an insult, "rotten toilet," which she invented herself. Mike, her young gorilla friend, was "Mike nut" when she felt jealous of him. Ron Cohn, Penny's coworker and the person who disciplined Koko, came in for the worst abuses. "Stupid devil devilhead" was an expletive for him. One day when a teacher asked Koko to tell her something funny, she did. "Koko love Ron," she signed, and kissed him on the cheek—then she chuckled. She liked the irony of her own jokes.

Koko could be moody, but she could also be endearing. When Mike was having his picture taken, she told him, "Smile."

Koko liked words. She caught on to pig Latin when workers resorted to it to disguise words like "candy." She also rhymed words. Part of her training consisted of hearing the spoken word when her teachers signed. Asked one day if she could sign a rhyme, she replied, "hair bear" and "all ball."

She was a wizard at inventing new words. After drinking her juice through a long rubber tube one day, she called herself an "elephant gorilla." A cigarette lighter was a "bottle match," and a mask was an "eye hat." A ring was a "finger bracelet."

Several years ago Koko, Mike, Ron and Penny moved to the country, where the gorillas could behave like gorillas. Today Koko and Mike climb fruit trees and eat the pears, plums, apples and apricots. Each has a modular building, an outdoor play yard and a computer that speaks. Here is a sign conversation between Penny and Koko after Koko had asked for more words on her computer:

> *Koko*: Do bean.
>
> *Penny*: Oh, she wants bean.
>
> *Koko*: Bad fake bird fake bird bird. Apple. (Koko uses the sign "bird" for word.)

At this point Penny realized Koko didn't want a bean but a being, a human being. She asked Koko if that was what she wanted.

> *Koko*: (excitedly) Do bean, do bean.

She was quite satisfied when the icon for human being appeared.

Koko is one of an endangered species. The foundation she inspired, The Gorilla Foundation, is dedicated to breeding gorillas in captivity. If all goes as planned, Koko will teach her own baby to sign, use a computer, and tell the "beans" more about themselves and gorillas.

THE HEMLOCK PAIR

A Living National Emblem

The wind twisted the white feathers on the heads of two magnificent bald eagles, the national emblem of the United States of America. Their yellow eyes were focused on two men crouched in their eight-by-ten-foot stick nest in an oak tree on the shore of Hemlock Lake in northwestern New York. The eagles cried in alarm.

Eagles mate for life. This pair, known as the Hemlock Pair, had raised young together for more than twenty years. This day in their big nest was one egg, which unbeknownst to them, was contaminated with chemicals. It would never hatch.

It was the year 1977, and the bald eagle was almost extinct in the eastern United States, primarily due to the chemicals ingested in their food. One of the chemicals, DDT, caused eagle eggs to be infertile or to crumble. Cities and highways deprived them of home sites.

The two men were part of the New York State Bald Eagle Recovery Program, the first such program in the United States. When they left the eagle nest that day, the Hemlock Pair circled overhead and disappeared.

Four days later, the eagles returned to find their egg gone and two eggs in its place. The men had removed the infertile egg and re-placed it with hawk eggs. A bird must go through the period of incubation to get its parental hormones flowing strongly enough to feed and brood young. The men hoped the eagles would incubate the hawk eggs; then, at the right moment, they would replace them with a live eaglet. The plan never got that far. The eagles saw the strange eggs and deserted the nest.

The next year the female laid another polluted egg. After the Hemlock Pair had been incubating it for almost a month, the men climbed back to the nest for a few minutes, then quickly departed.

When the Hemlock Pair returned, they found a two-and-a-half-week old bald eagle chick staring up at them. "Tarzan," as the men called him, had been hatched by captive eagles at the U.S. Fish and Wildlife Service's Patuxent Wildlife Research Center in Maryland. His worth could not be calculated. He was the hope of the many people trying to return the bald eagle to the American skies. Tarzan looked up at his foster parents, opened his beak and begged for food.

That did it. The hungry baby inspired the Hemlock Pair to pluck morsels from a fish they had stored and stuff the open mouth. Seeing that, the men stole away. The Hemlock Pair were going to be good parents.

They were right. In late June, Tarzan spread his huge

wings and sailed out over the lake and hills to independence. He was the first bald eaglet to be fledged from a wild nest in New York in five years.

The next year, the recovery team brought two eaglets to the nest too soon. The pair were not ready to feed and brood young, and they abandoned two eaglets. The men did not give up. A few days later they put a dummy egg in the nest. The pair looked at it, rolled it, then took turns incubating. In April they were ready to nurture, and when the men placed another eaglet in their nest, they raised it to independence.

In 1981 tragedy struck. The Hemlock male was shot. The recovery team was about to abandon their foster parent program when, in mid-March, the female surprised them by bringing home a new mate. He was a banded eagle from another New York State recovery program. He took up his duties as father, and together the two raised eight foster eaglets in the next several years.

When the female died at about thirty years of age, the

male found a new mate. DDT had been banned for almost ten years, and this female was not polluted. That year a completely new Hemlock Pair laid fertile eggs and fledged healthy young. The men's work was done. Wild eagles were raising wild eaglets again.

By 1991, thanks to the Hemlock Pair and the success of other recovery programs, New York had 189 bald eagles living in the wild. Seventeen pairs were raising youngsters.

Now, all across the United States and Canada where the bald eagle once reigned, state recovery programs are slowly bringing back from extinction this living symbol of the United States.

There is nothing more thrilling than to watch a bald eagle sail across the sky.

Bibliography

BALTO

The Baltimore Sun. February 4, 5, 6, 7, 1925.

Barbour, Ralph Henry. *The Boys' Book of Dogs.* New York: Dodd, Mead & Company, Inc., 1929.

Casey, Brigid, and Wendy Hough. *Sled Dogs.* New York: Dodd, Mead & Company, Inc., 1929.

Davidson, Margaret. *Seven True Dog Stories.* New York: Hastings House, Publishers, 1977.

The New York Times. February 1, 2, 3, 4, 8, August 27, 1925.

Standiford, Natalie. *The Bravest Dog Ever: The True Story of Balto.* New York: Random House, 1989.

PUNXSUTAWNEY PHIL

Pamphlet, Punxsutawney Chamber of Commerce, Punxsutawney, PA 15767.

"The Punxsutawney Groundhog." Punxsutawney Groundhog Festival Committee, Punxsutawney, PA 15767.

THE PACING WHITE MUSTANG

Ryden, Hope. *America's Last Wild Horses.* New York: E. P. Dutton, 1970.

SMOKEY BEAR

Pamphlet, United States Park Service, Washington, DC.

Tremain, Ruthven. *The Animals' Who's Who.* New York: Charles Scribner's Sons, 1982.

SCANNON

Cavan, Seamus. *Lewis and Clark and the Route to the Pacific.* New York: Chelsea House Publishers, 1991.

McGrath, Patrick. *The Lewis and Clark Expedition.* Morristown, NJ: Silver Burdett, 1950.

DeVoto, Bernard Augustine. *The Journals of Lewis and Clark.* Boston: Houghton Mifflin Company, 1953.

THE THREE GRAY WHALES

Palmer, Sarah. *Gray Whales.* Vero Beach, FL: Rourke Enterprises, 1988.

Thrush, Robin A. *The Gray Whales Are Missing.* San Diego, CA: Harcourt Brace Jovanovich, 1987.

Uiñiq, the Open Lead. Fall 1988. Vol. 2, Issue 2. North Slope Borough, Barrow, AK, 99723.

SUGAR

Green, David. *Your Incredible Cat.* Garden City, NY: Doubleday & Company, Inc., 1986.

Rhine, J. B., and S. R. Feather. *Journal of Parapsychology*, Duke University, 1962.

Tremain, Ruthven. *The Animals' Who's Who.* New York: Charles Scribner's Sons, 1982.

BLIND TOM

Howard, Robert West. *The Great Iron Trail: The Story of the First Continental Railroad.* New York: Bonanza, 1962.

————. *The Horse in America.* Chicago: Follett Publishing Company, 1965.

Tremain, Ruthven. *The Animals' Who's Who.* New York: Charles Scribner's Sons, 1982.

KOKO

The Gorilla Foundation Newsletter, 1992. Woodside, CA.

Patterson, Francine. *Koko's Kitten.* New York: Scholastic, 1985.

————. *Koko's Story.* New York: Scholastic, 1987.

————, and Eugene Linden. *The Education of Koko.* New York: Holt, Rinehart & Winston, 1981.

THE HEMLOCK PAIR

"New York's Bald Eagle Restoration Project." Albany, NY: Department of Environmental Conservation, 1992.

Nye, Peter E., and Michael L. Allen. "The Return of the Natives." *The Living Bird Quarterly*, Winter 1983.